CECILIA McDOWALL

VENI, CREATOR SPIRITUS

OXFORD

Commissioned by the Royal College of Organists in memory of Catherine Ennis (1955–2020)

Veni, Creator Spiritus

CECILIA McDOWALL

Gt.: 8', 2', Sw. to Gt.
Sw.: Diapason 8', Principal 4', Reed 8'
Ped.: Principals 16' & 8', Sw. to Ped.

© Oxford University Press 2023

Printed in Great Britain

OXFORD UNIVERSITY PRESS, MUSIC DEPARTMENT, GREAT CLARENDON STREET, OXFORD OX2 6DP
The Moral Rights of the Composer have been asserted. Photocopying this copyright material is ILLEGAL.

9
mp
f
12
15
Gt. + 4'
mf
Gt.
Sw.
+ Gt. to Ped.
18

21
Gt. + Mixture
f
Gt.
+ Gt. to Ped.
24
Gt. & Sw. Flutes 8', 4', Sw. to Gt.
Ped. Flutes 16', 8', Sw. to Ped.
27
mp dolce
30
mf
f

33
add to Sw.
add to Sw.
+ Gt. to Ped.
36
add to Gt.
add to Gt.
f
40
mf leggiero
Sw.
43
f

46
49
add to Sw.
f
Gt.
52
mf
Sw. mp
- Gt. to Ped.
+ Sw.
Reeds
Gt. p
+ Ped. Reeds
+ Gt. to Ped.
56

59
mp
f
62
add to Gt.
mf
65
Full Sw.
f
68
Full Gt.
poco rit.
ff
+ 32' if possible